Especially after not sleeping all night due to the very complicated sleeping arrangements of one Mr Blanket.

THE VERY F*CKING TIRED MOMMY

A Parody

Martyna Wiśniewska Michalak

unbound

First published in the UK in 2023
This edition first published in the United States in 2024

Unbound
Level 1, Devonshire House, One Mayfair Place, London W1J 8AJ
www.unbound.com

Text design by PDQ Digital Media Solutions Ltd

A CIP record for this book is available from the British Library

ISBN 978-1-80018-178-6 (UK hardback)
ISBN 978-1-80018-211-0 (UK paperback)
ISBN 978-1-80018-340-7 (US paperback)
ISBN 978-1-80018-179-3 (ebook)

Printed in China by C&C Offset Printing Co., Ltd

1 3 5 7 9 8 6 4 2

No dogs were shaved during the production of this book.

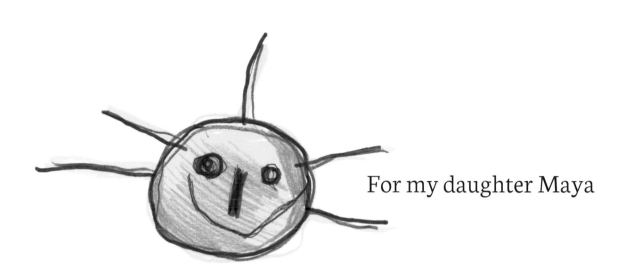

For my daughter Maya

In the light of the spring moon, a tired mommy lay on her bed, not looking forward to another week.

On Sunday morning, a little girl started
wreaking havoc around the house,
so with a heavy heart,
from the bed there emerged
a very tired mommy.

At once she started to look for coffee because otherwise the day would end really, REALLY badly.

And so the week went on...

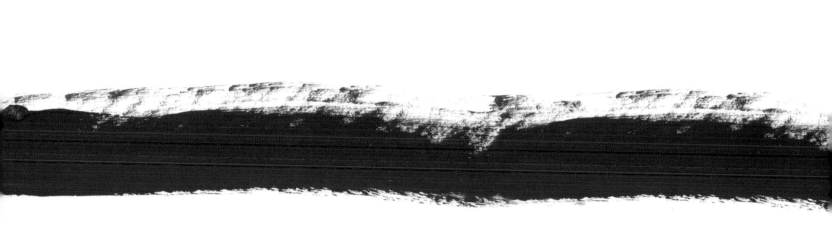

On Monday morning,
the kids put lipstick on the dog.

Mommy drank some coffee and
told herself that she could do it.
Little did she know...

She then ate a cookie,
but she was still hungry.

On Tuesday, the kids gave their toys a spa treatment in the kitchen sink. She had two chocolate bunnies with her coffee.

It's not that bad, she thought.

But she was still hungry, even though those bastards were 400 calories each.

On Wednesday, she ate three
popsicles after breakfast, but
she still craved something sweet.

Working from home with kids sucks.

She was tired.

On Thursday, she ate four cupcakes in fifteen minutes because the kids decided to cut their hair.

She added a glass of wine for good measure.

It was a good idea, but she was still tired and hungry.

On Friday, hiding in the bathroom, she ate five slices of pizza, but she was still fucking hungry. And really annoyed.

That day the kids shaved the dog.

On Saturday, the kids announced that pants were now optional.

She gave up and ate a slice of cheese, a rotting banana, a chocolate Santa from last Christmas, the kids' leftover lunch, half a jar of jam and a doggy treat (as she had no dignity left and had always kind of wanted to).

She finished it off with gin.

It was Sunday again.

That morning she had some herbal
tea and toast, canceled the limits on
screen time and felt much better.

She shut the bedroom door, told her kids to go ask Daddy, threatened death or injury to anyone who dared to trespass, and turned herself into a mommy-burrito.

She stayed inside all day and night. ALONE.

She drank some wine, watched a rom-com and talked to some friends. She slept without being kicked in the face.

And the next day...

She started all over again, because moms are awesome and they get shit done.

And even though sometimes they stress out, overeat or sleep all day, it's OK. We all need a way to vent and cope, and self-care is as important as caring for others.

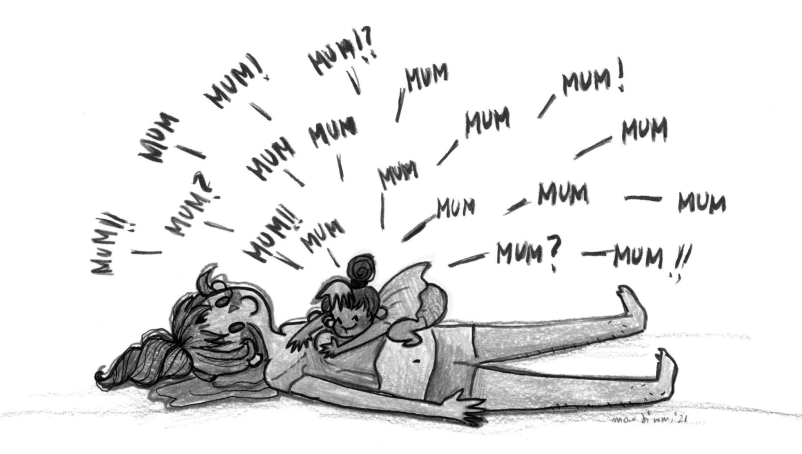

A Note on the Author

Martyna Wiśniewska Michalak is a painter, illustrator and doll maker. A graduate of the Academy of Fine Arts in Warsaw, she also writes and is quite good at generally staying alive. She is a mom of one, and likes naked cats and yuzu fruits.

Unbound is the world's first crowdfunding publisher, established in 2011.

We believe that wonderful things can happen when you clear a path for people who share a passion. That's why we've built a platform that brings together readers and authors to crowdfund books they believe in – and give fresh ideas that don't fit the traditional mould the chance they deserve.

This book is in your hands because readers made it possible. Everyone who pledged their support is listed below. Join them by visiting unbound.com and supporting a book today.

Hooda Abdullah, Lani Abels, Louise Absolom, Nicola Absolom, Anna-Maria Adaktylos, Natasha Adams, Lulu Al-Sabah, Gemma Albus, Melissa Allen, Steve Allen, Rob Alley, Chloe Allum, Lorna Allum, Adriana Almeida, Nicky Amy Louise, Tash Anderson, Colin Anderton, Christina Angeloudes Happy Birthday!, Stephanie Anger, Angie and Dan, Kana Aoyama, Theresa Aponte, Amanda Appleby, Nicole Appleby-McIvor, Bill Baker, Emmanuela Bakola, Jennifer Ballinger, Dorothee Barall, Barb007, Amanda Barnes, Laura Barnes, Harriet Bartelli, Helen Bartlett, Anna Batchelor, Anthony D Baynes, Ryley and Paige Beddoe, Samuel Beer, Angela Behm, Donna Bekendam, Graeme Bell, Sophie Bell, Phillip Bennett-Richards, BenSen, Stefanie Berger, Jeannette Bergmann, Sarah Berry, Agnieszka Biedrycka, Julian Birch, Richard Birdsall, Keely Blackwell, Peter Blunsdon, Julia Bochkis, Crystal Bonham, Severine Bonini, Alan Booker, Kelly Boswell, Corinne Bouchard, Mary Bownes, Pierrick Boyer, Kathyrn Boyes, Natalie Bradbury (Mummy to Poppy), Kieran Brady, Elissa Brae, Karin Brandner, Katja Braun, Rebecca Brennan, Loraine Bridges, Ash Brown, Naomi Buckingham, Dani Budde, Anjela Bugher, Valentina Buj, Natalia Buldrini de Amilibia, Emma Bull, Burim #NDS, Angela Burrows, Sally Butcher, Jamin Butler,

Bre Campbell, Katie Campbell, Louise Carbone, Vanessa Carpenter, Rob Carr, Yvie Carrick Gorham, Ann Carrier, Emma Castle, Rich Catlett, Amy Cavanaugh, Barbara Ceska, Lindsay Chamberlain, Gabriela Chambers, Claudia Chandler, Rachel Chapman, Kristofor Chappel, Debbie Chaston, Annekathrin Chatterjee, Gretchen Chiu, Mondoni Chung, Claire, Joanna Clark, Geraldine Clarke, Natalie Clinnick, Zoé Coade, Johanna Cobb, April Cohen, Emma Cole, GMark Cole, Charlotte Cole-Dalton, Brenda Conover, Hila Cooper, Stephanie Cooper, Tina Coventry, Haylie Cox, Ali Creasey-Benjamin, Stef D'Andrea, Bernie 'the jet' D'Lam, Maarten Daalder, Casa Dalton, Petra Damerau, Eley Davill, Blanca "Didi" Davis, Jezreel Davis, Natalie Dawes, Michael Dean, Stephanie Debrebant, Kirsten Deenik, Jen Dell, Shaneel Deo, Judith Devins, Sarah Di Battista, Laura Dingel, Crystal Doochin, Ben Dooks, Simon Drovs, Wendy Duri, Michal Durys, RJ Dymke, Louise Easaw, Jan Eckhoff, Rob Edwards, Martin Eggleston, Sabine Elbers, Ellicia Elliott, Anne Marie Ellis, Lisa Engel, Sarah Engel, Bonnie Eslinger, Beth Espey, Jan Esser, Sarah F J Jones, F*cking Tired Dad, Lisa Fabiny, Birgit Fahrni, Kelly Fairbairn, Janine Falk, Ewan Farry, Diane Fefferman, Lauren Feingold, Katy Ferdini, Kyle Ferrara Gallo, Jennie Finch, A. Findeklee, Sina Fischer, Virginia Fitzgerald, Molly Flatt, Nina Flieger, Steve Foote, Daisy Ford-Downes, Katherine Foster, Mrs M Fox, Maria Foy, Rebecca Francis, Gael Fraser, Monika Frauendorfer, Rachel Freedman, Sophie Freestone, Lisa Freydag, Ingrid Fuller, Helen Gale, Mark Gamble, Sarah Gamson, Jennifer Gandy, Holly Ganley, Rebecca Gann, Katarzyna Garbino-Anton, Ravpreet K Garrett, Rachel Gasper, Melanie Gebert, Anne Geese, Jamie George, Lyn Gibson, Sarah Gillam, Dominic Gittins, Carole Glover, Victor Glynn, Tarryn Godfrey, Greg Golsan, Dimarie Gonzalez, Alison Goodall, Sandra Goodman-Perkins, Maria Götten, Chris Gough, Katja Grach, Claire Grant, Clare Green, Paula Green, Georgia Greer, Heidi Gregory, Anna Groves, Katy Guest, Upuli Gunasinghe, Jemma H E Lee, Friederike Hachmeier, Quinn Hagedorn, Tiffany Hagood, Debra Hall, Jo Hammond, HannahWebb, Ben Harding, Pearl Harding-Hao, Julie Hardisty, Alice E Hargrave, Rachel Harper, Hannah Hartenberg, Christopher Hassall, Dirk Haun, Natasha Hayleigh Bowman, Vera Heidkamp, Ilka Heinen, Richard&Andrea Heming, Stefan Henning, Amanda Hepple, Janine Hermes, Anna Herve, Beth Heyeck, Amanda Hickling, Dawn Higgins, Carol-Lynn Hill,

Gwanita Hill, Jennifer Hill, Sriayuna Hilmi a.k.a Chunky Potato, Anna Hind, Nicholas Ho, Peter Hobbins, Carolin Hobert, Sabine Hofmann, Silke Hohmann, Stephanie Horn, Heather Horrocks, Bryan Howington, Joshua Howlett, Paul Huber, Keri Hughes, Chris Hurst, Konrad I Malgorzata, Jide Ihenacho, James Ireland, Charmaine Irwin, Lois Ismael, Lynn Iuliano, Lauren Jackson, Rajneesh Jain, Kylee Jay, Christian Jeffery, Helen Jeffries, Jennifer, Iris Jöbstl, Alison Johnson, Louise Johnson, Petra Johnsson, Jonas, Micah, and Frankie's Mom Cole, Ken Jones, April Joy, Kerryn Joyce, Andrea Junghans, Kai Alan Gonzalez's mum, Lucy, Diana Kaiser, Len Kantorov, Hannah Kapelj, Malina Kaplan, Phee Kear, Nerissa Keeler, Kate Kells, Martin Kieler, Jocelyn Kielhafner, Dan Kieran, Sonja Kießler, Danielle Kilpatrick, Heather Kingsley, Pamela Kirby, Kristen Kirchner, Johanna Klampfl, Sandra Kleiner, Cathérine Klonki, Mamá Klopse, Callie Knight, Doreen Knight, Rachel Knight, Linda Knowles, Melanie Koenig, Helen Kondos-Sheppard, Ela Kotliar, Katharina Kowalczyk, Anke Kremmling, Asya Krilcheva, Sabrina Kronschnabl, Sophia Krüger, Sarah Kuhlmann, Katja Kühnemundt, Kathrin Kunze, Kevin Kwan, Jacqueline Kyle, Ashley L-M, Veerle L., Annabelle Laborier-Saffran, Ralph Lachmann, Laura Lai, Christine Lallemand, Julie Lallement, Ralf Lang, Valerie Langfield, Lisa Lankshear, David Lannan, Meisoon Lau, Marcie Lawton, Allison Lee, Cindy Lee, Sze Min Lee, LeeAnne Leland, Tracy Levitt, Martin Levy, Anne Ley, Valentina Lilliu, Theresa Lim, Linda, Natalie Lissette, Sally Livermore, John Lloyd, Annika Loci, Andrea Loeffel, Niels Lohmann, Miriam Lohrengel, Steve Lomax, Emmanuel Lopez, Racheblue Love, Antonia Lovett, Jenna Luhrmann, Anke Lütz, Mike Lynd, Lynn, Rebecca Maas, Rob MacAndrew, Tara Macarthur, Leah MacDonald, Fiona Mackenzie, Ivana Mairhofer, Maja, Majo, Jesse en Millie, Kim Makk, Mama of Silvia & Szerene, Megan Manassero, Edith Mang, Deepa Manthravadi, Allison Marchalonis, Amelia Maria, Manuela Marischka, Christopher Martin, Jen Maskell, Phil Mason, Marion Mattausch, Cullen Matthew, Laura Matuszek, Anja Mayer, Laurie-Beth McCarthy, Caitlin McCleary, Lawrence McCrossan, Jemma McDonald, Amy McElhatton, Patrick S. McGrath, Sarah McGrath, Shelley McKaysmith, Elizabeth McKenzie, Kate Mckenzie, Rae McLean, Louise Mcleish, Chiara McNabb, Clair McNamara, Kate McNamara, Mindy Meehan, Ineke Meijer, Melinda Mendez, Anne Mertens, Quinnie Mignola,

Sarah Millington, Victoria Milner, Margot Minderjahr, Rob Minter, Emily Mitchell, John Mitchinson, Andreea Mogovan, Deepika Mokkarala, Niamh Moloney, Kate Monteath, Dorothy Moore, Laura Moore, Cate Moralee, Cheryl Ashton Moran, Alexandra Morel, Skye Morgan, Stephanie Moris, Simon Morris, Olga Mostinsky, Manuela Motyl, Sandra Muench, Laila Mühlhausen-Schneider, Laura Muir, Nora Müller, Robin Mulvihill, Rie Nagumo Tellerup, Cassi Nantes, Cecilia Nardi, Rachel Nash, Femke Naudts, Carlo Navato, Devin Neal, John New, Jo Newby, John Nguyen, Minh-Tam Nguyen, Kim Nguyen Fonua, Hoang Nhan, Joli Nichols, Amy Nicholson, Chris Niewiarowski, Erin Noel Braaten, Mairtin O'Riada, Keavy O'Shea, Kate O'Brien, Emma Odering, Kristina OK, Christina Olga Lozano, Jessica Orleman, Lindsay OSullivan, Sam Osys, Emily and Axl Owen, Marie Oxley, Jeremy Pak, Pamela, Valerie Pant, Jessica Paquette, Sam Parcher, Karin Parker, Sarah Jane Parker (my splendid friend), Liz Parsons, Katrin Patzelt, Noni Payling, Katie Pekkonen, Zubaidah Pereiras, Gehann Perera, Kelly Perkins-Douglas, Hugo Perks, Jessica Persico, Andrew Peterson, Marian Pickett, Emma Pilgrim, Mark Pinto, Fleur Pisano, Jac Pleass, Justin Pollard, Marion Pollinger, Connie Pople, Rou Poulakis, Aimee Pourroy, Jonathan Powers, Grace Prestia, Judith Price, Ernesta Prievelyte, Sarah Pring, Mike Pugh, Danielle Quina, Sean Raffey, Deepa Ramesh, Melanie Rankine, Roget Ratchford, Susie Ray, Michael Reason, Simon Rees, Alexandra Rehfeld, Erika Reid, Johanna Reiter-Pinto, Alex Rejstrand, Omer Reshef, Paul M. Reynolds, Tammy Reynolds, Elyse Ribbons, Emily Richards, Jamie Richards, Sally Richardson, Derek Richford, Tara Riddle, Sara Roach, Tinna Robertsdottir, Lorna Robertson, Louis Robertson, Catriona Ronke, Sheridan Rose, Ailish Roughan, Madison Royal, Alyssa Royce, Sarah Royle, Britni Ruiz, Darby Ruoss, Melanie Rush, Dominique Russell, Team Ruwitch, Megan Saad, Alex Sabo, Sarah Samuels, Erin Sandral, Kira Sass, Beata Sawicz-Gugala, Chauntel Scarr, Monica Schauweker, Carolina Scheffer Reque, Janina Schenk, Steffi Scheunemann, Robin Schinnow, Claudia Schirmeister, Sandy Schirmer, Manfred Schmiedl, Raphaela Schneider, Stefan Scholz, Claudia Schröder, Nelly Schubert, Anna Schürenberg, Hella Schuster, Saskia Schwagenscheidt, Katie Scotland, Amy Sedgwick, Liz Sedlmeier, Kristen Seely, Alina Seifriz, Janetta Seithe, Serena and Scott, Heather Scrignese, Emma Sharp, Remy Sharp, Nicholas Shaw, Christie Sinden,

Debra Slater, Keith Sleight, Ebony Smith, Emma Smith, Zoe Smith, Sarah Sparham, Genevieve Speegle, Serena Spencer-Jones, Kathrin Spieker, Rosamund Spiers-King, Teresa Squires, Cathy Stait-Gardner, Jason B. Standing, Carolin-Sophie Stängle, Jennifer Stazaker, Grant Stephens, Brooke Stewart, Michael Stewart, Robert Stickland, Lou Stirna, Lizzy Stokes, Helen Stone, Megan Straney, Miriam Strohmayr, Bronwyn Stuart, Elinor Styles-Davis, Helen Sucher, Paul Sugden, Soraya Summerfield, Susi, Katy Sutton, Martin Sweeney, Rae Sweeney, Matthew Sylvester, Christina Tackett, TanjAndreas, Philipp und Antonia, Chris Tanner, Leslie Tark Carver, Jane Teather, Sarah Tedjasukmana, Olivia Telfer, Gulya Ten, Evelyn Tenne, Heather Thomas, Lucy Thomas, Mary Thomas, Sarah Thomas, Jennifer Thompson, Jenna Thoms, Tia, Dani Tibbott, Sharon Tibbott, Brian Tilley, Katharina Tillmanns, Abigail Tobin, Tom and Liz, Monica Toohey, Michelle Torba, Jane Tostevin, Christina Trampnau, Silvia Treschau, Nina Treutler, Alexis Trittipo, Julie Tse, David G Tubby, Karen Turner, Davina Turner-Perkins, Johanna Uhrich, Uitje, Letisha Ulmer, Uris, Sani Valentine, Svenja van de Potvismodus, Caroline van de Vijver-Guldenmund, Sophie van den Belt, Norbert van Kampen, Dawn Van Taylor, Susanne Vellmer, Daniel Verinder, Iris Viken, Nefeli Vlahopulos, Stephanie Vogel, Gabriel Von dem Bussche, Katharina von Herff, Imke von Koschitzky, Esther W., Charlie Walker, Jill Walters, Fiona Wan, Bridget Ward, Claire Ward, Genevieve Ward, Brian Warren, Stuart Warren, Marta Wass, Cheryl Watkins, Sharon Webb, Stefanie Weber, Wiebke Weber, Jack Weeland, Pamela Welsh, Sabine Wenham, Jonathan Westwood, Krista Whalen, Rob Wheeler, Eline Wilke Michel Fiene Henrike, Sarah Willett, Ross Williams, Samantha Williams, Susan Willie, Kat Wilmott, Natalie Wilson, Karissa Wingate, Nastassja Wiseman, Jakub Wisniewski, Mateusz Wisniowski, Doris Witowski, Juana Wolf, Timm Wolf, Kayla Wolstenholme, Andrea Wong, Brianna Wood, Ashley Wood Munk, Stephanie Woods, Norelle Woolley, Jess Wotske, Vicki York, Jackie Young, Carolina, Olivia T i Agnieszka Ziatek, Julian Zimmermann, Marco Zink, <'((><